LIVING THINGS

ROBERT SNEDDEN

Mammal

FRANKLIN WATTS
LONDON • SYDNEY

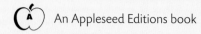
An Appleseed Editions book

First published in 2007 by Franklin Watts
338 Euston Road, London NW1 3BH

Franklin Watts Australia
Hachette Children's Books
Level 17/207 Kent St, Sydney, NSW 2000

Created by Appleseed Editions Ltd,
Well House, Friars Hill, Guestling,
East Sussex TN35 4ET

Designed by Guy Callaby
Edited by Pip Morgan
Illustrations by Guy Callaby
Picture research by Su Alexander

ISBN 978 07496 7556 1

Dewey Classification: 599

A CIP catalogue for this book is available from the British Library.

Picture acknowledgements

Title page Joe McDonald/Corbis; contents page Anup Shah/Nature Picture Library; 4 Robert
Landau/Corbis; 5t Merlin Tuttle/Science Photo Library, b Doc White/Nature Picture Library;
6 Anup Shah/Nature Picture Library; 7t Terry Andrewarth/Nature Picture Library, b Nigel J.
Dennis;Gallo Images/Corbis; 8 Lynn M. Stone/Nature Picture Library; 9 Doc White/Nature
Picture Library; 10 Wolfgang Kaehler/Corbis; 11t David Tipling/Nature Picture Library, b Hanne
& Jens Eriksen/Nature Picture Library; 12 D. Robert & Lorri Franz/Corbis; 13 Lucasseck/ARCO/
Nature Picture Library; 14 Justine Evans/Nature Picture Library; 15t Doug Allan/Nature Picture
Library, b Kim Taylor/Nature Picture Library; 16 Anup Shah/Nature Picture Library; 17t Anup
Shah/Nature Picture Library, b Bernard Walton/Nature Picture Library; 18 Joe McDonald/
Corbis; 19 Gary Braasch/Corbis; 20 Louie Psihoyos/Corbis; 21t Bengt Lundberg/Nature Picture
Library, b Colin Preston/Nature Picture Library; 22 Jeff Vanuga/Corbis; 24 Karl-Heinz Haenel/
Corbis; 25 Hans Reinhard/Zefa/Corbis; 26 T.J.Rich/Nature Picture Library; 27t Bruce Davidson/
Nature Picture Library, b Mark Carwardine/Nature Picture Library; 28 Photowood Inc./Corbis;
29t Mary Plage/Oxford Scientific Films, b Wolgang Kaehler/Corbis.

Front cover: Tom Brakefield/Corbis

Printed in China

Contents

What is a mammal?

Perhaps mammal isn't a word you've heard before, but you've certainly seen a few! Many people keep mammals as pets – for example, hamsters, guinea pigs, mice, cats and dogs. There are also mammals on farms, such as sheep, cows, pigs and horses. And if you really want to take a good, close-up look at a mammal just go to the mirror – because you're one, too.

BELOW *Cows and other farm animals are among the most familiar of mammals. Humans have had close relationships with them for thousands of years.*

Marvellous mammals

There are around 4,600 different types of mammal in the world. They come in many shapes and sizes, from tiny shrews to the mighty blue whale, the biggest animal that ever lived. There are mammals that can fly and there are mammals that can dive down into the deepest parts of the ocean.

What do all these wonderful animals have in common? Most of the mammals we see are furry, but do all mammals have hair or fur? What about whales and dolphins? You might think that all mammals give birth to live young and take care of their offspring. Would it surprise you to know that there are mammals that lay eggs?

WOW!

The smallest mammal in the world is Kitti's hog-nosed bat, also called the bumblebee bat. It measures just over three centimetres long and weighs about two grams.

WOW!

The biggest mammal, the blue whale, may be more than 24 metres long and weigh over 150 tonnes. The biggest dinosaur was only 60 tonnes in comparison!

Members of the mammal club

We feel closer to mammals than to any other type of animal, perhaps because we are mammals ourselves. They give us companionship; we use them in our sports; they provide us with food and clothing; they help us on our farms and carry heavy loads for us. In this book we'll find out more about our closest relatives in the natural world and discover just what makes a mammal a mammal.

Fur and hair

Rub the top of your head and you'll feel one of the special things about mammals that make them different from other animals. They all have fur or hair.

There is actually no difference between hair and fur – we just have two names for the same thing. Wool is hair, too. Hair grows from the skin and is made of a substance called keratin. No other type of animal has hair. Birds have feathers, and fish and reptiles have scales but none of them has a single hair. All mammals have at least some hair. Even dolphins have a few bristles around their blowholes. Some mammals are very hairy indeed.

Hairy coats

The coats of most mammals are made up of different kinds of hair. Close to the skin is the underfur, which is thick and soft. The outer coat is made up of the longer and coarser guard hair, which gives protection.

A mammal's hairy coat keeps it dry as well as warm. The skin makes an oily substance called sebum, which covers the hairs and waterproofs them. The fur of a polar bear is so thick that even when it swims its skin stays dry.

RIGHT *This orang-utan mother and her baby have coats of reddish-brown fur. The fur of a newborn orang-utan is almost orange, but gets darker as the animal grows older.*

Changing coats

Mammals shed hairs all the time, as you will know if you keep one as a pet! New hairs continually replace old ones. Some mammals change practically their whole coats at certain times of the year. For example, the Arctic hare sheds its white winter coat in the springtime, changing into its darker-coloured summer coat. This process of changing coats is called moulting.

Special hairs

Some hairs don't look much like hair at all. The horns of a rhinoceros are made of very tightly packed hair. The spines of a hedgehog and the quills of a porcupine are huge guard hairs. The whiskers of a cat and other animals are special hairs that are longer and stiffer than normal hairs. They are very sensitive to touch. Otters use their whiskers to detect fish swimming nearby in the water. The pangolin is an unusual mammal that appears to be covered in scales. But they are hairs that have become very flat.

ABOVE *A polar bear has a thick fur coat that protects it from the icy chill of the waters in its Arctic habitat. This bear was photographed in Hudson Bay, Canada.*

LEFT *The pangolin hardly looks like a mammal at all. What appear to be scales are special hairs.*

Keeping warm

All animals need to keep their bodies at the right temperature to work properly. Mammals can control their temperature by generating heat inside their bodies. They get this heat energy from the food they eat.

Wolves can generate heat from the food they eat in the same way as other mammals. They remain active hunters even in the depths of winter.

Active animals

Mammals are warm-blooded and can keep their bodies at a fairly constant temperature whatever the weather. This means they can be active even in cold conditions. Birds are the only other animals that are warm-blooded. Reptiles and amphibians rely on the heat of their surroundings to get warm.

The need to generate heat from their food means that mammals have to eat more than other animals. When a mammal is active, some parts of its body, such as the muscles, make more heat than others. The warmth is spread evenly through the body by the mammal's blood, which is pumped through the network of blood vessels by the heart.

Warm and hairy

Mammals that live in cold places often have great shaggy coats to keep them warm. Their fur traps a layer of air next to the skin. Heat doesn't travel well through air so this layer stops the heat from escaping quickly and helps to keep the animal warm.

Every hair is attached to a small muscle. These muscles can raise and lower the hairs to let air flow through the fur. When you're cold you've probably noticed goosebumps on your skin. These appear when the muscles pull on the hairs to trap air to make you warmer.

Layer of fat

Mammal skin is thicker than the skin of other animals. It also has a layer of fat underneath that keeps the heat in. In whales and other marine mammals this fat is called blubber. Water is much better than air at taking heat away, so the layer of blubber is much thicker than the layer of fat in land mammals. Water-living mammals also have bigger appetites than land ones and they can turn their food into energy much more quickly.

Sea otters blow air into their fur as they groom themselves. This is trapped in the fine down fur and provides a warm insulating layer of air next to the skin. The waterproofed guard hair keeps the skin dry.

WOW!

The thickest fur of any mammal belongs to the sea otter. More than a hundred thousand closely packed hairs in each square centimetre of skin keep the otter warm, even in the coldest seas.

Keeping cool

Mammals need to avoid getting too hot and they have a variety of ways for cooling off on a hot day or after a burst of activity.

One way a mammal can lose heat is by increasing the flow of warm blood through the blood vessels closest to the surface of their skin. The heat can then escape more easily into the air. When a mammal tries to save heat the opposite happens – it reduces the flow of blood through the skin.

BELOW *An Indian elephant sprays itself with water as it bathes in a river in Sri Lanka.*

Most mammals don't sweat and so have to lose heat in other ways. Some lick themselves all over so their saliva does the same job as sweat. Some mammals, such as dogs, cool themselves by panting. They lose some moisture from their lungs and this cools their bodies from the inside. Elephants and some other mammals cover themselves with wet mud on a hot day. As the mud dries out it cools the animal down.

Heat storage

Mammals that live in deserts, where it is particularly hot and dry, cannot lose heat by evaporation because it is important not to lose water. Many small desert mammals live in burrows where they hide from the heat of the day, only emerging at night when it is cooler. Camels can store heat in their bodies during the daytime and cool down again at night. They do not sweat or pant because they would lose precious water.

ABOVE *Dogs, such as this Irish setter, cannot keep cool by sweating. Instead, they lose heat by panting.*

Drying off, staying cool

Another way for a mammal to lose heat is through evaporation. This is what happens when a puddle dries up. The water in the puddle goes into the air and, as it does so, it carries heat energy. Some mammals have structures in their skin called sweat glands. These produce a liquid called sweat that covers the skin when the mammal is hot. As the sweat evaporates it carries away heat energy and so cools the mammal down.

WOW!

Why do elephants have big ears? Not to hear better, but to keep cool. An elephant's ears are filled with blood vessels that allow excess heat to escape into the air.

ABOVE *Camels live in dry desert conditions and so cannot afford to use valuable water to keep cool. They can store heat in their bodies during the day and then cool down at night.*

Walking, running and jumping

Mammals move from place to place in many different ways. Most mammals, such as cats, cattle, dogs and deer, move around on four legs. A few, such as kangaroos and humans, move on two legs.

Moving forwards

Mammals put their feet on the ground in different ways. Some, such as shrews, bears and humans, put the whole length of their foot on the ground with each step. These animals often have thick skin on the soles of their feet.

Others, such as dogs and cats, walk on their toes. As they move forwards their wrists and heels never touch the ground. Thick pads behind the animal's claws give protection and extra grip. Some of the swiftest running animals, such as deer and horses, move on tiptoe. Tough hooves protect the animal's toes. The hooves, claws and nails of mammals are made of keratin, like their hair.

When they walk forwards, most four-legged mammals first move one front leg and then one back leg on the opposite side. Camels and giraffes, however, move both legs on the same side at the same time.

LEFT *Like humans and bears, raccoons place their feet flat on the ground as they walk along.*

Picking up speed

A mammal can move very quickly when it is in a hurry and starts to run. When a horse gallops there is a moment when all its legs are off the ground at the same time. We had to wait until the invention of high-speed photography to see this because it happens so quickly. A cheetah arches its flexible spine as it runs so that its hind legs can land in front of its front legs. This means that it goes forwards in a series of rapid springing leaps.

Jump to it

A few mammals jump rather than walk. Kangaroos and jerboas (small, mouse-like animals) propel themselves forwards using their big back legs and feet. Their tails help them keep their balance. Jumping is a very effective way of moving around. A kangaroo can cover six metres or more in one leap.

WOW!

A cheetah can sprint at just over 100 kilometres per hour but only for 200 metres or so. Over long distances no animal can catch the pronghorn antelope. It can sprint nearly as fast as the cheetah and can keep going at a speed of 60 kilometres per hour.

HOW A KANGAROO JUMPS

A kangaroo, with its powerful back legs and big feet, is so well adapted to leaping that it cannot walk. It uses its big strong tail to help it balance as it jumps.

Swinging, swimming and flying

**Some mammals don't keep their feet on the ground.
These are the mammals that have taken to the trees,
spend their lives in the sea or even fly through the air.**

Kings of the swingers

Many mammals are at home in trees. Squirrels have sharp claws
and flexible legs that help them run up and down tree trunks.
Most monkeys and apes are excellent climbers. With their long,
powerful legs, and strong grasping fingers and toes, they can launch
themselves from branch to branch, high above the forest floor.

Gibbons are masters of swinging through the trees, moving
effortlessly from one handhold to another. They can leap nine
metres or more between branches or run lightly over the tops
of branches while holding their long arms out for balance.

*This male white-handed gibbon
hangs effortlessly poised in a
tree in a national park in
Thailand. It seems ready to
swing off at a moment's notice.*

Water life

Seals and walruses spend a lot of time in the water and are ungainly animals on land. Their legs are called flippers and are shaped like broad paddles. Some seals propel themselves through water by moving their back flippers quickly from side to side. Others swim with their front flippers. All these mammals are so highly adapted to life in the water they find it difficult to move around on land.

Whales and dolphins are mammals that have completely adapted to life in the sea and never come on to the land at all. Unlike fish, which move their tails from side to side, whales and dolphins swim by moving their tails up and down.

ABOVE   *The Antarctic leopard seal is slow and ungainly on land, but in the water it is a fast and efficient hunter.*

Taking to the air

A flying squirrel can glide for long distances between trees. As it leaps it opens large flaps of skin between its front and back legs. Together, these flaps act like a parachute, keeping the squirrel in the air for longer. The animal steers itself in the air with its tail.

Bats are the one type of mammal that really can fly. Their wings are formed by thin skin stretched tightly between their long fingers. This skin is also attached to the ankles. The wings of a big bat, such as a flying fox (which isn't a fox at all, of course), can be a metre and a half across. Most bats are much smaller than this.

LEFT   *This flying squirrel can glide for about 100 metres from one tree to another if it starts from a high enough perch.*

Mammal eyes

Sight is a very important sense for mammals. It helps them to find food and to spot a predator that might be about to make a meal out of them.

Two eyes, two pictures

Try this experiment. Hold up a pencil and look through one eye only while you line up the pencil with a distant object. Then, without moving the pencil, look through the other eye instead. The pencil and the object are no longer lined up. Each eye shows you a slightly different picture of the world. By combining the pictures your brain can judge distances between objects. This is called binocular vision.

RIGHT *The eyes of the impala, a type of antelope that lives in Africa, are set well back on each side of its head and provide good all-round vision.*

LEFT *Hunters, such as this Bengal tigress, have binocular vision that allows them to judge the distances to their prey.*

The hunters and the hunted

How much of the world an animal can see at any one time is called its field of vision. Looking at a mammal's eyes can tell you something about its field of vision and the sort of life it leads. Hunters, such as lions and tigers, have eyes on the front of their heads. They have very good binocular vision because it is very important to know how far away its prey is before it makes a leap. Leap and miss and you go hungry. Monkeys, squirrels and other tree-living mammals have good binocular vision, too, so they can judge their leaps from branch to branch.

Mammals that are hunted by other animals need to be constantly on the look out. Their eyes are on the sides of their heads, giving them a good all-round field of vision. A rabbit can see almost all the way around.

Seeing in colour

Do mammals see in colour? No one seems to know for sure. But since we are mammals, and we can see colour, it is a fair bet that others do as well. However, mice, rabbits and dogs don't appear to see the colour red. The problem is that so much of seeing goes on in the brain. Really, you'd have to be a giraffe or an antelope to know what these animals see.

BELOW *A chimpanzee's view of the world is very similar to our own. Both humans and chimpanzees have binocular vision and see the same range of colours.*

Mammal ears

Mammals have an excellent sense of hearing. Many of them have hearing that is much better than ours, and some mammals can hear sounds that we cannot.

Outer ears

The flaps on the side of your head that we call ears are just the outer part of the ears. They help to concentrate the sound and direct it to the inner part of the ear. Try cupping your hands just behind your ears to make the collecting area bigger. Can you hear a difference? Many mammals can move their outer ears around, swivelling them towards the direction a sound is coming from.

LEFT *The large ears of the black-tailed jackrabbit are excellent sound detectors. They alert the animal to the slightest noise.*

How an ear hears

Hearing starts when sounds travel down to the eardrum, which is like a very thin skin across the middle part of the ear. Sound waves make it vibrate like a drum skin. A chain of three tiny bones (the hammer, anvil and stirrup) on the other side of the eardrum passes the vibrations to the inner part of the ear. Here, the different sound vibrations are sorted out and sent to the brain as nerve impulses. The ears of birds, amphibians and reptiles only have a single bone.

WOW!

As well as being the biggest animal the blue whale is also the loudest. A blue whale's low-pitched call is louder than a jet aircraft and can be heard hundreds of kilometres away.

THE HUMAN EAR

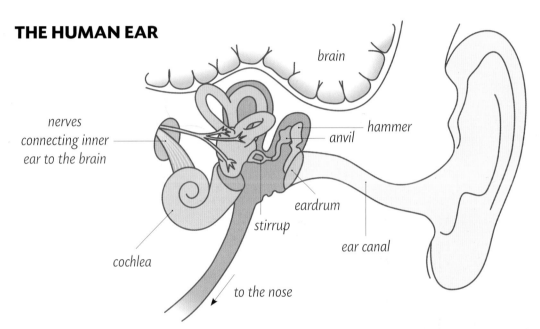

brain

nerves connecting inner ear to the brain

hammer

anvil

eardrum

stirrup

ear canal

cochlea

to the nose

The ear is much more complicated than it looks from the outside. Deep inside, the cochlea has 10,000 hair cells that turn sound vibrations into electrical signals. These are sent via nerves to the brain.

Echoes and high-pitched sounds

Mammals such as bats can make and detect sounds that are too high-pitched for us to hear. Most bats are active at night. How do they know where they are going as they fly around in the dark? The answer is that they use sound.

As a bat flies it continually makes high-pitched sounds, which are called ultrasounds. When the ultrasounds hit an object, the echoes bounce back to the bat's ears. These echoes help the bat to build up a picture of its surroundings in sound. This system of detection is called echolocation. It is so accurate that a bat can tell where an insect is, how big it is and the direction in which it is flying.

Whales and dolphins that swim in the dark depths of the ocean also use high-pitched sounds and echo detection in the water.

ABOVE *The fleshy structure on the nose of this spectral bat is thought to help focus the high-pitched sounds it uses in echolocation.*

Scents and tastes

For many mammals their most important sense is neither seeing nor hearing but smelling. The ability to detect the faintest of smells in the air can be the difference between life and death.

Getting up your nose

All mammals, humans included, have openings called nostrils on their face. Inside the nostrils are scent detectors that are sensitive to tiny amounts of chemicals in the air. Some mammals have better detectors than others. Humans aren't particularly skilled at picking up scents; a dog's scent detectors are hundreds of times better.

LEFT *Bloodhounds have an incredible sense of smell. They can track someone by following a scent trail that may be several days old.*

Scent has many meanings to a mammal. Predators sniff the air for the scent of a meal. Others are alert for the predator's scent to avoid becoming that meal.

Most mammals produce different kinds of scent themselves. Many use scent as a way of marking their territory, the area they defend against rivals. A hippopotamus sprays dung to make smelly marker posts; cats, such as lions and domestic cats, use their urine. Some mammals have scent detectors that are especially sensitive to the smell of the opposite sex. This helps them to find a mate.

Tongues and tasting

Smelling and tasting are very similar senses. Both involve detecting different chemicals. The difference between the two is that smells can be detected at a distance but something has to be touched to be tasted. The tongue is the taste-touching organ. Its surface has a number of detectors that can pick out different tastes. The sense of taste helps an animal to decide whether or not something is good to eat. Rats, for example, have a very good sense of taste and learn to avoid things that have made them unwell.

ABOVE *Beavers make scent-marking posts by scraping together piles of mud and plant material, which they then smear with a smelly substance.*

ABOVE *A brown rat feasts from a sack of grain. It avoids eating anything that tastes bad.*

WOW!

The ratel, or honey badger, of South Africa produces a suffocating scent that stuns bees in their nests. The ratel then enters the nest and helps itself to the honey.

Biting and grinding

Amphibians, reptiles and fish have teeth. So do mammals, but theirs are different. The teeth of most other animals are all alike, but mammals have a variety of teeth to suit the food they eat.

Milk teeth

Mammals are the only animals to have two sets of teeth in their lifetimes. Young mammals do not have teeth when they are born. The first set to appear are sometimes called milk teeth. As the animal grows older the milk teeth are replaced by another set, called the permanent, or adult, teeth.

A roaring grizzly bear reveals its impressive teeth. It eats a varied diet of berries, fish, squirrels and even insects.

Meat-eaters

Some mammals, such as bears, weasels, cats and dogs, have jaws that move up and down and teeth that are suited to eating meat. At the front of the mouth are sharp, blade-like teeth called incisors that can scrape the meat from bones. Next to these are the large pointed canine teeth that hold and kill the animal's prey. At the back of the mouth are the carnassial teeth. The top and bottom sets of carnassials come together like shears to cut flesh and crunch bones.

BEAR TEETH

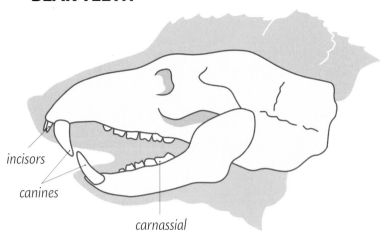

incisors

canines

carnassial

Plant-eaters

Some plant-eaters only have incisors in the lower jaw. These bite against a strong pad in the upper jaw as they snip through grass and other plants. The cheek teeth at the back have flat tops and are close together, making a large surface for grinding tough plant material. The jaws move from side to side to help the grinding process. Cheek teeth are constantly worn down and so grow throughout the animal's life.

incisors

cheek tooth

HORSE TEETH

HUMAN TEETH

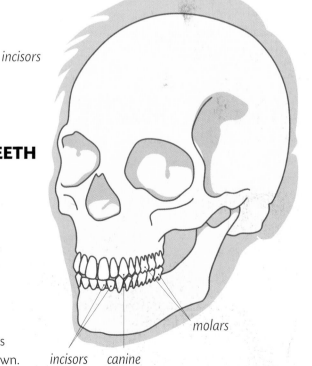

A varied diet

The teeth of mammals with a varied diet, such as humans, are somewhere between those of a meat-eater and a plant-eater. Their jaws can move up and down and from side to side. Rodents, such as rats, mice and beavers, have chisel-shaped incisors on their upper and lower jaws. These are ideal for gnawing through tough foods, such as nuts. A rodent's incisors also grow throughout its life as they are always being worn down.

molars

incisors   *canine*

Mothers and babies

Nearly all female mammals give birth to live young. Some mammal babies can walk almost as soon as they are born, while others are more helpless. All of them rely on their mothers for food.

Mother's milk

Female mammals are unique in the animal world. All other animals have to catch or gather a supply of food for their young, but female mammals can supply their own. They have special organs called mammary glands that produce nourishing milk. The number of mammary glands varies from one type of mammal to another. Human females have two, female dogs can have three to five pairs and some rats can have as many as 12 pairs.

BELOW *Some mammals have more young than others. This female pig has seven piglets that compete for her milk.*

RIGHT *The duck-billed platypus is one of the world's more unusual mammals. It lays eggs rather than giving birth to live young.*

The young mammal feeds on the milk its mother produces by sucking on a nipple, or teat. The milk contains all the food it needs – fat, protein, sugar, vitamins, salts and water. Smaller mammals, such as mice and rabbits, may only feed their young on milk for a few weeks, but the young of bigger animals, such as elephants, rely on the milk for a few years.

A risky journey

Some young mammals have a difficult time getting to their mother's nipple. The young of marsupials, a group of mammals that includes kangaroos, koalas and wombats, are born blind and very small. A newborn kangaroo weighs less than a gram. After it is born the tiny animal has to crawl up its mother's body to find a nipple. It can only use its front legs as its back legs are still too weak. Once it gets there it will remain attached to the nipple for up to two months while it grows and gets stronger. Many marsupials have a special pouch that protects the young mammal as it grows.

Egg-laying mammals

Three kinds of mammal lay eggs instead of giving birth to live young. These are the duck-billed platypus and two types of spiny anteater. All three live in Australasia. The duck-billed platypus lays two eggs in a burrow, but the spiny anteaters lay a single egg and keep it in a special pouch.

When the eggs of these mammals hatch after about ten days, the young feed by licking milk from a special patch of skin on the female's belly.

WOW!

The mammal mother with the richest milk is the seal. Seal milk is over 50% fat (human milk is about 4%). The baby seal needs this fat to build up its layer of protective blubber.

Growing up

One of the things that make mammals different from other animals is their intelligence. Mammals are the quickest and cleverest animals on the planet. For a young mammal, part of growing up is learning the skills it needs to survive.

ABOVE *A young wildebeest gets to its feet almost as soon as it is born. This is important as lions and other predators may be nearby.*

Parental care

Some young mammals can move on their own from a very early age. Within a few hours of being born most young hoofed mammals, such as horses and wildebeest, struggle to their feet and follow their mothers. This is very important because the young animal is vulnerable and in danger of being eaten by predators.

RIGHT *Cape hunting dog puppies keep a watchful eye for adult dogs returning to their den with food.*

Other young mammals are practically helpless for some time after they are born. Their mother is their most important carer as she is their source of food. In a few cases – for example, many monkeys and apes, and predators, such as wolves – the father also helps to look after them until they can fend for themselves.

Sometimes a group of animals share the responsibility of looking after the young. African hunting dogs live in packs and all the adults, not just the parents, bring food back to feed the young pups hidden safely inside the den.

Weaning

As the young mammal grows and develops it must switch from a diet of mother's milk to eating adult food. This period, when the mother stops feeding her young with milk, is called weaning. It happens earlier for some mammals than others. Young rabbits feed themselves at around three weeks old, whereas elephant calves may not be weaned for four years.

During the weaning period the young mammal learns how to be an adult, often by copying what its mother and other adults do or by playing with other youngsters. An adult cat brings small animals to the den for her kittens to practise their catching skills, for example. Female otters push their sometimes unwilling offspring into the water so they can get used to swimming.

Eventually, the young mammal is ready to live as an independent adult. Of all the mammals, we take the longest to reach this stage.

WOW!

Whales, like all mammals, need to breathe air. Young whales are born in the water and are helped to the surface by their mother so they can take their first breath of air.

Top mammals

Mammals have lived on the Earth since the time of the dinosaurs. Over the last 60 million years they have successfully spread to every habitat on the planet.

Mammals live everywhere, from the shores of the Antarctic to the ice caps of the North Pole and in every desert, forest, grassland and mountain range. Many mammals spend all or part of their lives in the water. Whales and dolphins inhabit every ocean, from the tropics to the polar regions. Mammals live in the coldest and hottest of places, on land and in the oceans.

BELOW *There are more humans on Earth than any other mammal. Six billion people live on the planet.*

WOW!

The largest known mammal colony in the world is the colony of 20 million or more Mexican freetail bats in Bracken Bat Cave, Texas. The largest human city, Seoul in Korea, has just over ten million people.

ABOVE *The Javan rhinoceros is close to extinction. There may be fewer than a hundred left in the wild.*

What makes a mammal?

All mammals share three things which distinguish them from other types of animal. First, the adult females produce milk to feed their young. Second, all mammals have at least some hair at some point in their lives. Third, and less obviously, mammals are the only animals with three tiny bones inside their ears.

Intelligent creatures

Mammals are more intelligent than other animals and we humans think we are the cleverest of all. Humans live all over the world because we can build shelters and make clothes that allow us to survive in all climates. Our varied diet allows us to take advantage of whatever foods are available and our ability to make and use tools has allowed us to change our surroundings.

Dangerous humans

We often seem to make these changes at the expense of our fellow mammals and other living things. Many mammals are close to extinction because we hunt them too often or destroy their habitats. The numbers of large animals, such as tigers and elephants, have fallen alarmingly. There may be fewer than a hundred Javan rhinos and Yangtze river dolphins.

Some people think that we might change the world so much that many mammals won't be able to live in it any more. And those mammals could include us. That really wouldn't be clever at all.

ABOVE *A group of lionesses scan the savannah for prey. When they hunt they work together to bring down their catch.*

Glossary

Adaptation   A feature of a living thing that makes it better suited to its particular life style; the flippers of a seal are an adaptation to a life spent mostly in water.

Binocular vision   Vision that combines images from both eyes to give a sense of depth and distance.

Blood vessels   Networks of tubes that carry blood around the body. Arteries carry oxygen-rich blood to the rest of the body; veins carry blood to the lungs to pick up oxygen and return blood to the heart.

Blubber   A thick layer of fat that protects mammals, such as whales, seals and polar bears, from the cold of the sea.

Canines   Large pointed teeth at the front of a meat-eating mammal's mouth. Canines are used to grip and stab the animal's prey.

Eardrum   The part of the ear that picks up sound vibrations travelling through the air.

Echolocation   The way that bats, whales and dolphins sense their surroundings by producing high-pitched sounds and detecting the echoes of those sounds bouncing back from objects around them.

Evaporation   What happens when a liquid turns into a vapour and carries heat energy away with it.

Extinction   The term that describes the death of every member of a particular plant or animal. Extinction means that the type of living thing has ceased to exist anywhere on Earth.

Field of vision   The area that an animal can see without moving its head.

Flippers   The broad, flat limbs of mammals such as seals that are adapted for swimming.

Guard hairs   The long, coarse hairs that form a mammal's outer fur.

Habitat   The place where a living thing makes its home.

Incisors   Blade-like teeth at the front of a mammal's mouth. Incisors are used for cutting.

Keratin   A strong, flexible material that is found in hair, horns, scales and feathers.

Lungs   The organ that larger animals, such as amphibians, mammals, birds and reptiles use to take oxygen from the air they breathe.

Mammary glands   Parts of a female mammal's body that produce the milk with which she feeds her young.

Marsupial   A type of mammal, such as kangaroos and koalas, in which the young are born very small and undeveloped.

Mate One of a pair of animals that produce young together; the pair is always male and female. Producing young is called mating.

Molars Teeth at the back of a mammal's jaws; the molars are used for crunching and grinding food.

Moulting Shedding old fur which is replaced by new growth.

Saliva A watery fluid produced inside the mouth to help with chewing and digestion.

Sebum An oily substance produced by the skin that keeps fur waterproofed.

Sweat glands Parts of the skin that produce sweat, a fluid that cools the mammal by evaporation.

Taste buds Tiny taste detectors, usually found on the upper surface of the tongue.

Territory The area in which a mammal or other animal lives. Many mammals defend their territory from others and leave scent marks to tell others where their territory is.

Ultrasound A high-pitched sound made by bats and other animals; the sounds cannot be heard by human ears.

Underfur The inner layer of short, fine fur next to a mammal's skin.

Warm-blooded A term that describes an animal that can generate warmth from the food it eats; mammals and birds are warm-blooded.

Weaning The process of changing a young mammal's diet from mother's milk to other foods.

Websites

http://www.bbc.co.uk/nature/animals/mammals/
Website based on the *Life of Mammals* television series – includes quizzes and games.

www.ucmp.berkeley.edu/mammal/mammal.html
The Hall of Mammals – information on the diversity of mammals.

www.afsc.noaa.gov/NMML/education/marinemammals.htm
About marine mammals – learn about the mammals that spend all or part of their lives in the sea.

http://www.marsupials.org/
Links to a variety of sites with lots of information about those unique mammals, the marsupials.

www.arkive.org/species/GES/mammals/
Information, including photographs and video clips, about the world's rarest mammals.

Index